C000284816

# CHICKEN

## by Eva O'Connor and Hildegard Ryan

## ‖SAMUEL FRENCH‖

written permission of the publisher. No one shall share this title, or part of this title, to any social media or file hosting websites.

The moral right of Eva O'Connor and Hildegard Ryan to be identified as authors of this work has been asserted in accordance with Section 77 of the Copyright, Designs and Patents Act 1988.

## USE OF COPYRIGHTED MUSIC

A licence issued by Concord Theatricals to perform this play does not include permission to use the incidental music specified in this publication. In the United Kingdom: Where the place of performance is already licensed by the PERFORMING RIGHT SOCIETY (PRS) a return of the music used must be made to them. If the place of performance is not so licensed then application should be made to PRS for Music (www.prsformusic.com). A separate and additional licence from PHONOGRAPHIC PERFORMANCE LTD (www.ppluk.com) may be needed whenever commercial recordings are used. Outside the United Kingdom: Please contact the appropriate music licensing authority in your territory for the rights to any incidental music.

## USE OF COPYRIGHTED THIRD-PARTY MATERIALS

Licensees are solely responsible for obtaining formal written permission from copyright owners to use copyrighted third-party materials (e.g., artworks, logos) in the performance of this play and are strongly cautioned to do so. If no such permission is obtained by the licensee, then the licensee must use only original materials that the licensee owns and controls. Licensees are solely responsible and liable for clearances of all third-party copyrighted materials, and shall indemnify the copyright owners of the play(s) and their licensing agent, Concord Theatricals Ltd., against any costs, expenses, losses and liabilities arising from the use of such copyrighted third-party materials by licensees.

## IMPORTANT BILLING AND CREDIT REQUIREMENTS

If you have obtained performance rights to this title, please refer to your licensing agreement for important billing and credit requirements.

# SUNDAY'S/CHILD

**Sunday's Child** is an award-winning Irish theatre company run by Eva O'Connor and Hildegard Ryan. We aim to make vibrant, contemporary work about issues that are often swept under the carpet. Our plays have toured Ireland, the UK, Australia, USA and mainland Europe. They include *My Name is Saoirse* (Winner of First Fortnight Award 2014, Argus Angel Award 2015, and Adelaide Best Theatre Award 2017) *Overshadowed* (Winner of Fishamble Award for Best New Writing 2015, and adapted for screen for BBC Three) *Afloat, The Friday Night Effect, MUSTARD* (co-produced with Fishamble The New Play Company, winner of Scotsman Fringe First 2019, Critics Circle Award Adelaide Fringe 2023 and adapted for screen for RTE Storyland) and most recently *Chicken*. Sunday's Child runs FUTURE LIMERICK: Climate Arts Festival in conjunction with the Lime Tree | Belltable in Limerick, Ireland.

*Chicken* premiered in Summerhall at the Edinburgh Fringe in August 2023, where it enjoyed a sellout run. It won the Filipa Bragança Award for best solo female/non-binary identifying performer and the Lustrum Award 2023. The performance was directed by Hildegard Ryan, with costume design by Bryony Rumble and lighting design by Marianne Nightingale. The cast was as follows:

**DON THE CHICKEN**. . . . . . . . . . . . . . . . . . . . . . . . . . . . . . . Eva O'Connor

The 2024 tour of *Chicken* was produced by Sunday's Child, and opened at the Traverse Theatre on 18th April.

# CAST & CREATIVE

## DON THE CHICKEN/CO-WRITER | EVA O'CONNOR

Eva O'Connor is an award-winning writer/performer from Ogonnelloe, County Clare, Ireland. She makes work for stage, screen and radio, and is co-artistic director of Sunday's Child alongside Hildegard Ryan. Eva is the writer of several published, award-winning plays. Her credits include *Overshadowed* (now a series on BBC Three), *MUSTARD* (Winner of Scotsman Fringe First 2019 and Critics Circle Award Adelaide Fringe 2023 and adapted for television for RTE Storyland), *HORSE PLAY* (produced by Glass Mask Theatre), *My Name is Saoirse*, *Maxwell House* (Dear Ireland for the Abbey Theatre), *Maz and Bricks* (produced by Fishamble the New Play Company), *Afloat* (co-written with Hildegard Ryan), and *The Friday Night Effect* (co-written with Hildegard Ryan). Eva won the Filipa Bragança Award for best solo female/non-binary identifying performer at the Edinburgh Fringe 2023 for *Chicken*. Recently she wrote on *Taigh Tŷ Teach*, a tri-lingual co-production with Fishamble: The New Play Company. She is also co-curator of FUTURE LIMERICK: Climate Arts Festival with Hildegard Ryan and Sophie Fuller. Eva runs *What's The Story*, a quarterly night of new writing at the London Irish Centre.

## DIRECTOR/CO-WRITER | HILDEGARD RYAN

Hildegard is an award-winning writer/director with credits in stage and screen from Skerries, County Dublin, Ireland. Hildegard is co-artistic director of Sunday's Child with Eva O'Connor. Hildegard co-wrote and directed the interactive play *The Friday Night Effect* and *Afloat*. Her directing credits include plays *My Name is Saoirse*, *Overshadowed* (adapted for BBC Three, co-written with Eva O'Connor), *Afloat*, *MUSTARD* (Winner of Scotsman Fringe First, Critics Circle Award Adelaide Fringe) and *Frigid* by Rosa Bowden (Winner of the Bewlays Little Gem Award). Hildegard has also directed extensively for TV including *MUSTARD* for RTE Storyland, *Casualty*, *The Dumping Ground*, *Still So Awkward* for Channel X/CBBC and she co-directed two episodes of *Dodger* for CBBC/NBC which won in the Children's Programme category at the RTS Awards 2023. She is also co-curator of FUTURE LIMERICK: Climate Arts festival with Eva O'Connor and Sophie Fuller.

## LIGHTING DESIGNER | MARIANNE NIGHTINGALE

Marianne "Maz" Nightingale is a lighting technician and lighting designer from South East England. Throughout her professional career she has worked as part of the lighting department in many London producing theatres such as the Royal Court, the Young Vic, the Bridge Theatre, the National and annually at the Edinburgh Fringe. It was her passion for new writing which led her to working with Sunday's Child. Marianne has been designing and touring with the company for almost ten years, working on a multitude of their award-winning productions: *My Name is Saoirse*, *The Friday Night Effect*, *Afloat* and *MUSTARD*. "*Chicken* has been a fantastic piece to work on. It's been a pleasure lighting this show and of course shining a spotlight on Don the chicken!"

## COSTUME DESIGNER | BRYONY RUMBLE

Bryony is a sculptural artist working mainly with fabrics, leathers, foams and forms. She is a props, costume props/creature fabricator for film, TV, opera, theatre and events. She studied Fine Art at Norwich School of Art and Design and then trained as a Cordwainer at The London College of Fashion, before finding a love for character design, puppets, masks and sculptural costumes through a more technical performing arts course, also at LCF. Bryony is interested in texture and form, manipulation of fabric and new silhouettes. She is a lover of things, and inspired by colour and clashing patterns, gaudy and kitsch, odd and macabre, grotesque and revolting and all that lies in between. Credits include: Igor Studios, KMFX, Warner Brothers, Millennium FX, Punchdrunk, Disney Theatrical, Significant Object, RSC, Royal Opera House, Glyndebourne, ENO, National Theatre, Shakespeare's Globe, Adam Spiegel and Kenny Wax Ltd.

# CHARACTERS

**DON THE CHICKEN**

# AUTHORS' NOTE

We initially wrote *Chicken* as a vegan call to arms. We thought that if we could get an audience to fall in love with a chicken, perhaps they'd think differently about their next meal. Writing a one-chicken show about a ketamine addicted actor cock always felt like a creative risk. There was a definite moment of "what have we done?" in the seconds before Eva stepped out on stage for the first time in the giant chicken costume in Summerhall in Edinburgh 2023. We were bowled over by the response to our wacky, troubled chicken friend. Don took on a life of his own and *Chicken* became a play about otherness, emancipation, rebellion and belonging.

*Ní saoirse go saoirse na sicíní.*
There can be no freedom until the chickens have freedom.

*Classical music plays. Enter* **DON** *the chicken. He pecks around, looking inquisitive and a bit anxious. He pecks the ground, pecks the audience and occasionally looks up, startled. He keeps pecking for a good two minutes.*

Ahhh I'm only messing.

I'm only winding ye up.

**DON** *pecks at a random man in the audience.*

Look at this lad here

and the fear in his eyes.

He thought it was gonna be

one full hour of

peck-peck-peck performance art.

No, I wouldn't do that to you.

My levels of celebrity self-delusion

are not quite there yet.

I'm no high falootin' conceptual artist.

I'm a simple storyteller

like the bards of yore.

I am a humble actore.

Hello my friends.

Thank you for coming!

Or rather...

you're welcome.

What a privilege for all of you

to join me here in my chambers.

Cosy,

claustrophobic,

almost like...chickens,

in a coop.

I know why you're here.

Couldn't resist a glimpse of me

in the pimply flesh.

The feathered dynamo,

the tabloid prince,

Don Murphy.

Godfather to Michael Fassbender's three children.

Once bedfellow to Martin Scorsese – don't ask.

Celebrant at Pamela Anderson's ninth wedding.

A lowly bird from the Irish back of beyond,

now the world's most famous cock.

Perhaps you're here

out of some strange,

carnivorous compulsion

to consume me.

Not with your mouths

but with your eyes.

Or perhaps you were dragged in here

against your will.

Entrapped,

ensnared,

in a cruel twist of fate.

Regardless of your reasons

I'm thrilled to have you all here

with me tonight.

After years of guarding my privacy

with my short chicken life,

the time has come

to share my story.

Why now? I hear you ask.

Well, simply put – death.

I know it sounds morbid,

but the end is nigh.

You may think that we are different,

you and I,

my feathered friends,

but death is coming for all of us.

In fact, it is very literally

just around the corner.

Where to begin.

Born in the south of Ireland,

a Kerry cock through and through.

Hup the kingdom!

I hail from Caherdaniel,
home of Daniel O'Connell,
the great liberator
after whom I am named.
He fought for the rights
of peasant Irish Catholics
way back when.
He was an Irish freedom fighter
much like myself.

I was born a free-range chick
on a windswept Kerry sand dune.
Egg cracked open
under the crunch of human foot.
Shell split down the middle
like a fault line
by none other than
my future surrogate mother
Máire Murphy.

There I am staring up at her,
my neck nearly broken,
the son she never had.
But of course poor Máire
is riddled with the guilt
of having stepped on me
in her sensible Clarks shoes
and her terrible '90s perm.

She takes me home
to nurse me back to full health.
I am so tender in those early days
that her husband Declan
wants to whisk me into an omelette.
But Máire is having none of it.
She takes me under her wing,
gets an actual prosthetic wing made,
God bless her.

As a young chick,
I beg Máire to take me back
to the sand dune of my birth.
To the scene of the shell squashing crime.
But Máire is wounded,
thinks I'm longing for my chicken mother
and so we avoid that beach
like the plague.

It's not long 'til Declan too
takes a shine to me.
He kits me out in the Kerry colours,
determined that I too will play a bit of GAA
like the other boys.
But the sight of a Gaelic football
coming towards me
strikes fear into my veins
and I freeze

as the lad I'm meant to be marking
boots the ball clean over the bar.

*Useless Chicken shit!*
Cries the crowd from the stand.
Declan rushes onto the pitch,
whisks me to the sideline,
perches me on his knee,
and clucks,
*You are named after Daniel O'Connell*
*the great liberator.*
*You are not a chicken,*
*you are a proud Irish man*
*and my son.*

My first foray into performance
comes when I am cast as Jesus
in the nativity play.
Now I'm sure they're thinking
the rooster's not up to much.
Let's stick him in the manger,
fling a tea towel on top of him
and he'll probably sleep through most of it.
But I give everything to the role.
The crowd are awed.
When they look upon the manger,
they see not a chicken

but the actual Christ child.
I suppose you could say
that discovering Jesus
changed my life.

Soon after feathers are ruffled
when I announce that I'm flying the nest.
Headed to New York City
in search of my big bird break.
Máire weeps,
*Oh God Don,*
*I can't bear to think of you all alone*
*over there in the big smoke.*
Declan is stoic.
Emigration has been the fate
of many an Irish man.
Why should his son be any different?
*Well lad, not a hope in hell*
*you'll make it as an actor over there*
*but sure, God loves a trier.*

Those early days in New York City are tough.
I'm living claw to beak,
not a scrap of fat on my breasts,
sleeping rough on window ledges.
It is then that Paulo the pigeon
pecks his way into my life.

A Glaswegian bird
with an unhealthy obsession
with Celtic football club
and bread.
Paulo takes me bin diving
outside the city's finest bakeries.
He plunges beak first
into trash cans that smell
like rotting corpse,
emerges victorious
with still warm loaves of brioche,
bagels soft as snow.
We perch on the nearest bench
and chow down
until we have heart palpitations.
I confide in Paulo.
I share my deepest fears and insecurities.
I tell him about my refusal to fly
for fear of revealing
my most chickenish traits.
My desperation to make it as an actor
in the big smoke.
Paulo locks eyes with me,
his mouth full with day old poppadom.
*In 1967 Celtic won five trophies.*
*Five!*

*Is that no inspiring?*
*Let that be a lesson to you my wee pal.*
*Anything's possible,*
*anything!*

Soon after I find an agent
in the Yellow Pages
and present myself at his office
in Washington Heights.
He's a small man in a wife beater
with more hair on his arms
than I have feathers on my wings.
*Books are closed!*
he barks, without even looking up
from his newspaper.
But I have heard it
on the grapevine
that he has a weakness
for a bit of bird.
And although I am young and scrawny,
I scrub up well.
I am aware even then
of the intoxicating allure of my plume.
When the agent finally clocks me
his eyes flare with desire.
*Well, well, well...*
*I feel like chicken tonight!*

My stomach churns
at his slur.
*Can you squawk baby bird?*
*Come sit on my knee,*
*and show daddy how you squawk.*

I would love to tell you
that I hold my rooster head high
and peck my way right out of there.
But I am young,
I am desperate.
And so I flit.
I flutter.
I perch on his knee
and against my better judgement,
I squawk for him.
*Ka kawwww!*

Máire is a great believer
in guardian angels.
She says that the lord
stations them on earth
in places you would least expect.
And I certainly didn't think
that mine would come to me
in the form of a naked Michael Fassbender
on a film set.

My hairy armed agent
has landed me a role
in Fassbender's latest feature.
Now my part is minuscule.
It's a fly-by.
Literally.
I'm an extra in a scene where Michael
runs naked through a chicken coop
letting it all hang loose.
*Very on brand for Fassbender*, says you.
They've wrangled myself
and two other amateur birds
for the scene.
A pair of hens from upstate New York.
Our instructions are very simple:
*As soon as you clap eyes on his pecker,*
*run like the wind!*
But the hens are nervous.
I say
*Listen girls,*
*the director already thinks*
*we're a bunch of bird brains.*
*Let's prove him wrong.*
But my pep talk
only makes them overthink.

As soon as they hear

the snap of the scene board

they freeze,

hens in the headlights.

The director is furious.

Cuts them from the scene.

So it's just myself and Fassbender

going for a take.

*And action!*

In he comes,

big swinging micky.

And on cue I scatter and run like bejaysus.

**DON** *runs around squawking.*

But not before I slip a quick glance to camera.

A smize.

An imperceptible wink.

*That chicken's really got something*

says the director watching the rushes.

Fassbender too is impressed.

*Nice work lil fella,* he says.

*Not so bad yourself Micheál!* I say,

clapping him on the back

with a sweaty wing.

*Wait,* he says.

*You're Irish?*

*Oh, I am begorah.*

*A fellow Kerry cock!*

Fassbender waves me into his trailer,

pours me a hefty glass of Jameson.

*If you don't mind me asking, lil fella,*

*what exactly is the craic with you?*

*Are you a hen or a chicken?*

*Cockerel or a rooster?*

Now listen my feathered friends,

I'm well used to this line of questioning.

People,

all of them,

are perverts.

Always mad to get the details

on the genitalia.

I say

*Listen Michael*

*I am much more than a meagre bird,*

*I am a humble actor, much like yourself.*

*I am a proud Irish man,*

*I am Declan's son*

*and most of all...*

*I'm anything you want me to be.*

    **DON** *winks at him.*

Michael raises his glass

*Just as well you don't identify as a bird.*

*Have you seen the lunch menu?*

It is then that I learn,

they're serving my two friends

from upstate New York.

Their necks broken,

speckled feathers plucked,

deep fried and slathered

in hot sauce.

*I suppose,*

says Michael,

*when they say*

*"no animals were harmed*

*in the making of this motion picture"*

*it doesn't always extend*

*to the catering truck.*

I can feel tears pricking behind my eyes.

But I can't cry,

not in front of Fassbender.

So I laugh –

*hahahaha!*

*Well Micheál,*

*less competition for me,*

*amirite?*

Michael and I get pissed drunk
in his trailer that afternoon.
Him plying me with Jameson,
me singing –
*The auld triangle*
*went jingle jangle...*
Him saying,
*Christ you're like a little slice of home.*
*There's something about you*
*that just takes me back to the four green fields.*
*Trasna na dtonnta,*
*dul siar, dul siar.*
*I like you, d'you know that?*
*Birds of a feather we are.*

The following week,
in true guardian angel style,
Fassbender calls me.
Tells me he's got an idea
up his sleeve for a feature.
Thinks it has huge potential.
*I'm thinking a load of cocks*
*pecking the shit out of each other.*
*A grim, visceral take*
*on violence, consumerism, sex.*

*At the end you realise*

*that the main rooster has*

*hallucinated the entire thing.*

Cockfight Club *we'll call it.*

I'm sure most of you have seen it.

I won't bore you with the details.

But that film changes everything for me.

It's my big bird break,

big as the New York skyline,

life smashed into smithereens kind of break.

My career a golden egg.

Me dubbed:

*A fresh hatched star.*

*The chick who changed cinema.*

*British bird soars to new heights!*

Interesting isn't it

the way every Irish personality

becomes British overnight

as soon as they achieve

anything of note.

*A Bird's Life.*

*A Cock's Tale.*

*Babe: Chicken in the City.*

*Birdies of Inisherin.*

*Flight Plan.*

*Fly Away Home 3, 4, 5* and *6.*

I work like a dog,

like a horse.

No, let's repurpose the phrase.

I work like a chicken

for three straight years.

Lights.

Camera.

Action.

Scenes, scenes...

*Incredible scenes altogether!*

says Máire, when she rings me

every Sunday like clockwork

to check in.

*I heard you turned down the knighthood,*

says Declan

*That's my boy, that's my feckin' boy.*

*Would you not come home for a holiday Don?*

says Máire

*We could do the ring of Kerry,*

*go for an aul scone in Killarney.*

*Ah Máire, sure the man is working.*

*And anyway, holidays are for soft lads.*

*Well Don,* says Máire

*as long as you're happy.*

But that, my feathered friends,

is the problem.

I am not.

I'm Everest heights

of roost ruling fame

but inside I'm destitute.

The carcass of my life is

cracking under the weight

of its own emptiness.

I'm a blinkered bird,

working myself to the chicken bone.

Convinced that if I pause,

even for a second,

the golden egg of my career

will be snatched out from under me.

One day on the set of *Angry Birds*

Colin Farrell takes me aside.

He says

*Listen bud,*

*you need to let them feathers down*

*d'you hear me?*

*Otherwise they're gonna start fucking falling out.*

I know he's right.

So that night, reluctantly,

I get dolled up

for a party at Colin's place

in the foothills of LA.

The bouncer on the door

is a massive lad draped in a tri-colour.

Inside there is a keg of Guinness

with my name on it,

literally.

But despite Colin's thoughtful touches of home

I feel alien,

an awkward, vulgar bird

in a sea of glamorous humans.

I catch sight of my reflection

in a gilded mirror.

My scrawny chicken legs,

beak so glaringly large,

eyes so beady and bulging.

Colin senses my discomfort,

siphons me off from the crowd.

He leads me by the wing

into a marble bathroom,

where like a cheeky butler boy

he presents me with a silver tray

of powdered white lines.

Now my feathered friends,

at this point I am still

a good, naive, repressed,

little catholic boy.

But Colin works his best Mrs. Doyle on me,

*Ah go on, go on, go on,* he says.

*A bird like you could do*

*with a bitta horse tranquilizer*

*in his veins.*

That first line.

The burn of it.

The thrill of it.

As though Colin has opened a sliding door

into a parallel universe

in which I feel absolutely fuck all,

and it is bliss.

> *Music begins to play.* **DON** *sniffs a line and starts to come up on ketamine. He dances, cautiously at first, and then slowly gets into the groove. As the music blares, his dancing becomes more unhinged. He flails manically, trips and falls flat on his beak. The music stops abruptly.*

I trip on my way out of that party

at Colin's place

in the foothills of LA

and tumble beak-first

into a years deep K-hole.

I suppose you could say that night

with Colin and the ketamine

draws a powdered white line
down the centre of my life.
Cuts it clean in two
with a credit card into
before and after.

The next chapter is a
hazy, ketty cloud of
well... euphoria.
And that, my feathered friends,
is the problem with addiction.
It will destroy you –
but not before it shows you
one hell of a good time.

The ketamine instills me
with a reckless abandon
I have never known.
Oh, and it gifts me with a sex life.
I have always been drawn to women
of the humanoid variety.
Their long-limbed allure
intoxicating to me.
But I had lived in fear
of rejection, mockery.
Hated the sight
of my naked pimply body.

Couldn't stand the fact
that I was such a...
chicken.

But now with the ketamine
coursing through my veins,
I see myself in a whole new light.
I am a virile rooster
ready to sow my wild oats
across the fields of New York City.

I gobble up women
like they are chicken feed.
I hop up on anyone who will have me.
Actors, PAs, bartenders, vets.
I have a particular penchant for vets.
There's Samantha
who has a small animal practice
on the Upper East Side.
Joan who works with
larger animals upstate.
Macey who nurses me
back to full health
when I break my wing
on the set of *Star Wars*.
Let's just say Macey knows a thing or two
about chicken anatomy.

Macey knows her way
around the body of a bird.
But I am ashamed to say
that I'm only with her
for access to the supply chain.

And look,
we've all had a slutty era.
Sexual emancipation is to be celebrated,
particularly if you're Irish.
But I'm not proud
of my promiscuous period.
I meted out rejection
to my own kind.
Ignored even the hottest of hens.
Declan's words ringing in my ears:
*You are not a chicken*
*but a proud Irish man*
*and my son!*
as I swiped left
on the city's most beautiful birds.

Then comes the Oscars.
The nom nom nomination
for best supporting actor
in a gritty remake of
*The Birds*.

It's the pinch me, pluck me, slap me
stuff of dreams.
There is war over who will dress me.
I eventually settle on a
brilliant white Versace tux
and I feel like an elegant Irish Elvis.

I am nervous
on the day of the ceremony.
True to form
I devour a rake of lines.
I'm so sky high when they call my name
that the win barely registers.
As I step up
to accept the tiny statue of dreams,
I feel a strange sensation
in the centre of my face.
There are audible gasps from the audience,
cameras on me like flies.
I look down to see rivers of blood
snaking down
my brilliant white Versace tux.
I think
*Christ on a bike*
*an ill-timed nosebleed.*
But it is much, much worse
my feathered friends.

My beak has detached itself from my face

and is lying in a pool of my own blood

on the Oscars stage.

Reese Witherspoon is rushing towards me

waving a single white tissue

and mumbling,

*Hunny, are you alright?*

*You want me to call someone?*

I'm thinking,

*Yes actually Reese.*

*That would be brilliant.*

*Could you give my dealer a buzz*

*and tell him I'll meet him outside*

*in ten minutes?*

*God knows I'm going to need a gram or two*

*after this bloody fiasco.*

But instead of rushing

beakless and ashamed

off stage,

I own the moment.

I go full Lady Macbeth.

*Out, damned spot:*

*out I say!*

*One; two.*

*Why then 'tis time to do't.*

*Hell is murky!*

But my little red-carpet improvisation

comes off as less inspired and

more unhinged.

And the next day,

beak sewn back on

and hanging by a literal thread,

I am sectioned.

Only Paulo the pigeon sticks by me

when I'm released from rehab.

He replaces my bags of ket

with bags of baguettes.

He fields concerned calls

from Máire and Declan.

He bathes me when he claims

I smell like rotting meat.

One day

when I'm lying in my penthouse

dreaming of the sweet relief

of relapse

he calls me.

*How's ma favourite*

*fucked up rooster?*

*C'mere pal*

*ah got tickets to see a show at MOMA.*

*Was meant to be going*
*with some bird*
*but now she's saying*
*she's washing her feathers.*
I know this is a lie.
Paulo has never organised a date
with anyone or anything
other than a pretzel.

*You're always banging on*
*that I should be more cultured.*
*Come with me, brother.*

So that afternoon I meet Paulo
in the foyer of MOMA.
He's wearing a faded Celtic jersey
and looks out of place
in the pretentious crowd.
He hands me a ticket
to a performance art installation named
FERTILIZED.
The gallery lights are blindingly bright.
They remind me of rehab.
All I can think of is fertilising my nostrils
with a line of K.
But then the lights dim,
the chatter dies.

A spotlight appears

in the centre of the room

on a strange boxy metallic machine

reminiscent of...

a sausage meat grinder.

A hen emerges from the crowd.

She's a delicate specimen.

She looks like a fluffy, white,

bird-shaped pom-pom.

Tiny feathers adorn her chicken ankles

as though she's wearing little flares.

She's a rare breed

and admittedly good-looking

– for a chicken.

The floor beneath her feet

starts to move –

a conveyor belt.

She's pacing now,

one foot in front of the other,

going nowhere fast.

The machine behind her judders to life,

a strange metallic whirring.

It's baying for blood.

Petals begin to rain down

from the MOMA sky

onto the hypnotic hen.

They're sucked backwards

into the metallic machine

and pulverised into a spattering red dust.

The conveyor belt speeds up now.

The hen is running

in an effort not to get sucked in.

She begins to moan,

a strange, guttural, animalistic noise.

*Naghhhhhhh neughhhhh...*

A girl behind me whispers

*Can chickens masturbate?*

The hen turns to expose

her fluffy white rear.

In the centre is

a tiny bullseye of pink.

Her chicken vagina!

I've never seen one before.

In all my years

of elaborate Pornhub searches –

strictly of the humanoid variety –

I have never clapped eyes on anything

so scandalously beautiful.

The audience gasps
as her pink ring widens
and a hard dome appears.
A creamy white entity.
She cries out
*KA KAWWW!*
Her egg is born!
A perfect thing of beauty,
expelled into the world.

She steps away from the conveyor belt,
leaving the egg exposed and trundling
towards the jaws of the machine.
There is no emotion in her beady eyes
as she watches it get sucked in,
as if in slow motion.
The audience recoil,
they retch
as they are spattered in liquified egg.

The hen produces a frying pan.
She is scraping the slime
of her own egg
off the floor,
off the walls.
I press my Pradas further up my beak
but tears are streaming down my face.

The grinding of the metallic machine

goes through me.

The déjà vu of it

punches me in the chicken gut.

Paulo grabs me by the wing,

steers me from the crowds.

*Galleries man.*

*No safe.*

An hour later Paulo and I

are recuperating

in a Vietnamese joint

a block from MOMA.

Me with my beak in a bowl of pho,

Paulo horsing into

a bánh mì across from me.

Suddenly out of nowhere:

*You're the cock who walked out of my show...*

I turn and there she is

the artist hen,

sipping a bottle of Tiger beer,

her performative chicken vagina

safely stashed away

under a pair of Lucy & Yak dungarees.

*Was it too real for ya? Too spicy?*

*Oh no!* I reply.
*No, your little period piece*
*didn't offend me at all.*
*I found it boring.*
*Tragically boring*
*and reductive.*
I lie, my feathers flustered.

*Oh, I see. How so?*

*Well I mean, a hen laying an egg?*
*What's next?*
*A chicken courageously*
*crossing the road?*

*Honestly, I don't really see*
*how you're in a position to*
*critique my work*
*seeing as you ran out of there*
*after two minutes like a*
*headless chicken.*

*I – I had to take a very important call from my agent.*
At the risk of sounding like a narcissist,
doesn't she know who I am?

*Well hunny, I'm Sadie.*
*Perhaps someday you and I*
*could have dinner*

*and you can cock-splain me*
*how to make my work less*
*reductive.*

A week later
I cross the threshold
into Sadie's Brooklyn loft.
She pecks me on both cheeks.
*Mwah mwah!*
*If it ain't the famous cock.*
We perch on hay bales
and Sadie serves me dried mealworm
in hand-thrown pottery bowls.
It's the simple, rustic food of her youth.
She tells me she was raised
in Dallas to be a show bird,
a prized White Silkie,
famed for their docile nature
and stunning good looks.
But Sadie just didn't have it in her
to be a good little show girl.
*My handler caught me*
*getting it on backstage*
*with a big-ass Malay rooster.*
*He was like four feet tall*
*practically a dinosaur.*

*After that I was out on the streets.*
*I plucked up the courage*
*to fly to New York.*
*It took me four days straight,*
*I was so tired I nearly fell outta the sky.*
*When I landed,*
*I got a job modeling for a life drawing class*
*in a little vegan café downtown,*
*and it was then*
*that I discovered the power of art.*

I am mesmerised by Sadie
and the frizzy white feathers
which frame her face.
*Look,* I say
*I would like to apologise for*
*my behaviour at FERTILIZED.*

*Oh hunny,*
*I get it from a lot of cocks.*
*The generational trauma*
*is a lot for you boys.*

I explain that I was born
a free-range chick,
raised in a loving and stable household
and that for me
trauma really doesn't come into it.

*Oh come on baby,*
*you're living through*
*the genocide of your own kind.*
*Every goddamn day*
*boys just like you are getting*
*gassed, pulverised, smushed to smithereens.*
*You're working as an actor*
*in a toxic, human-skewing industry.*
*You're a recovering addict.*
*You tryna to tell me*
*that you ain't traumatised?*
Sadie's beady black eyes meet mine
in what feels like a challenge.
As she approaches me,
I am petrified.
I almost consider taking flight.
*Oh hunny, don't look so scared,*
*I ain't gonna eat you.*

Now my feathered friends,
I'm sure you'd all love to know
the gory details.
But a chicken never kisses and tells.
Or in this case
mounts, mates and spills the tea.

But let's just say,

chick on chicken sex is very different

to the humanoid variety.

It's ironic really

that us cocks are a symbol of virility

when I don't even have one.

That's right,

I'm a cockless cock,

and I slide off Sadie's back several times.

But when we finally master the dance

it is magic.

Afterwards I lie on Sadie's hay bale

and weep.

*Oh hunny, don't cry.*

*You're home.*

Life with Sadie is in vivid technicolor.

She dials up the joy

on the switchboard of my life.

She scrawls me secret notes

in my scripts:

*To my favourite naughty cock...*

She is learning Irish on the internet

so she can serenade me

in my ancestral tongue

*Mo ghrá thú go daingean...*

Sadie's hold on me is chemical.

Falling for her is akin

to the head over heels descent

into addiction.

I live in fear

that she will rip the chicken heart

from my chest

and fling it into her MOMA meat grinder.

Sadie begs me to take to the skies with her.

But I refuse,

always desperate to conceal

my most chicken-ish traits.

*One day baby you're gonna fly free.*

*Mark my words,*

*one day I'm gonna see you*

*soar across that sky.*

Sadie's star is on the rise.

Galleries worldwide are clamouring

to book FERTILIZED.

But she boycotts all venues

who have the audacity

to serve animal products.

She organises "shit ins"

where hundreds of birds enter KFC

and stage a radical act

of mass bowel opening.

Sadie's friends are a raggle-taggle group of

parrots, pigeons, poultry.

They call themselves

activists,

disruptors,

change makers.

They pride themselves

on refusing to swallow injustice

which I find ironic

as they seem to sit around all day

smoking weed and downing bottles of Moët

which they have absolutely no issues digesting.

Sadie's best friend

is a pheasant named Freya.

She was raised

on a country manor estate in Sussex

by aristocrats who shot her

and then took her in

when she refused to die.

Freya corners me at a party.

It's a hippie shindig at Sadie's place.

There's so much incense burning

I feel like I'm being hotboxed

by an overzealous priest.

*Don, can I ask you something?*

says Freya.

*Why is it you're so apolitical?*
*Is it that you've no first-hand experience*
*of struggle?*
*Or are you just too chicken*
*to speak out?*

I slam down my champagne glass
with a force that surprises even me.
*Listen Freya,*
*you English pheasant!*
*You think I don't know struggle?*
*I come from nothing.*

*I work sixteen-hour days on set,*
*the only cock in the room,*
*proving to birds around the world*
*that they can be more than a piece of meat.*
*You want to talk politics?*
*Yeah, let's talk politics.*
*800 years my people suffered under your lot.*
*The famine –*
*inflicted by your ancestors on mine.*
*You have the audacity*
*to call me a chicken?*
*I am not a chicken!*
*I am a proud Irish man*
*and Declan's son!*

Afterwards Sadie approaches me
her beady black eyes
are brimming with disappointment.
*What the hell's your problem, Don?*
*Banging on about 800 years*
*like you're some kinda leprechaun cliché.*
*Look I get it,*
*the Irish were crushed by the English.*
*But can't you see*
*your own kind are getting crushed*
*every goddamn day?*
*Freya's not your enemy,*
*you've upset her.*
*She's crying in an Uber*
*on the way back to her brownstone!*
*Can't you see the bigger picture?*

Sadie is distant with me.
A gulf opens up between us
and it feels like an illness
worse than bird flu.
I start using again.
I sleep with Macey the vet.
I miss Máire's birthday
for no reason other than
I am a useless piece of chicken shit.

Paulo calls to my penthouse,

finds me crying

into a plate of ketamine.

*What you greetin' for you sad cock?*

*Get back out there and get that bird back!*

So I present myself

on Sadie's doorstep.

I get down on my scaly knees

and I beg for her forgiveness.

*Look Don,*

*it's not the drugs or the ego*

*or even the sex that I mind.*

*It's that you don't care!*

*You're always telling me*

*you're named after some great liberator*

*but you ain't willing to fight?*

The next day,

linked wing in wing with Sadie,

I attend my first ever

Birds' Rights Rally.

I am determined to prove to Sadie

that I can be the compassionate cock

that she deserves.

Hundreds of thousands of birds

descend upon New York City

to protest the wet markets,

where you can buy a chicken alive alive-o
and have it slaughtered
before your very eyes.
It doesn't get much fresher than that.

The air ripples with tension,
helicopters circle above
but Sadie is serene.
*Look Don, I know this ain't really your scene,*
*but you being here*
*and showin' us some solidarity –*
*it means the world to me.*

We march onwards.
The swelling crowd grows agitated.
As we descend upon the wet market
we sit down en masse.
We perch in rows of peaceful protestors,
a feathery blanket of birds
stretching for miles across Manhattan.
A hush descends momentarily,
but then feathers fly
when the NYPD swoops in.
They're cuffing kestrels,
chaining cocks,
grabbing birds by the neck
so hard that they might break.

Sadie is calm among the chaos.

*We gotta put our bodies*

*on the line baby!*

*This is how we win!*

But my resolve is weakening.

I'm due on set the next day.

I'm picturing me calling Hairy Arms from a jail cell.

Or worse still

him identifying my body

in the morgue.

The cops are closing in now.

They're battering birds

and breaking beaks.

But the flock refuses to take flight –

not a single bird budges.

There is a crack of a gunshot

and suddenly we are engulfed

in a strange blue smoke.

*Tear gas baby,*

*hold me!*

*We're gonna be alright!*

But in that moment

I do something

that surprises even me.

I spread my wings and take to the sky.

As I flap my feathers
I am surprised
by the weightlessness of my own body.
Sadie looks on, incredulous.
*Don, no!*
*Whose side are you on?*
As I ascend above the fray
Sadie becomes a tiny dot below.
I soar to safety
in the ultimate act
of betrayal.

The next day that image of me,
a solo bird across a tear gassed sky,
makes the front page
of *The New York Times*.
My inbox is flooded
with a deluge of hate mail
and death threats from my former flock.
Sadie is arrested
for "battering a police officer",
both her wings are broken in the fray.
I try and visit her
but she refuses to see me.
I plunge into a depression
darker than I have ever known.

I call Hairy Arms.
I tell him it's all over,
I'm withdrawing from public life.
I fling my phone and laptop out the window
of my fifth floor penthouse apartment.

I cut contact with Paulo.
I even consider paying a local butcher
to put me out of my misery.

Days later, Hairy Arms turns up
in person at my penthouse.
*My gawd,*
*you actors are all the same,*
*think you're so original*
*going off grid.*
*Why the hell do you never*
*answer your phone chick?*
*I got news.*
*Martin McDonagh wants you*
*for his latest feature.*
*He's doing* Chicken Run *the remake.*
*Brendan Gleeson's the farmer,*
*Colin Farrell is playing his wife.*
*They're filming in Ireland, Kerry,*
*that's your hometown, right?*
*Look, I'm gonna book you a cab*
*to take you to JFK.*

*I swear to gawd if you overdose*
*between then and now*
*I'll wring your neck myself!*

I have ten days at home
with Máire and Declan
before filming begins.
I lie on my bed,
like a teenage, emo chick
cursing south Kerry's nonexistent
supply of ketamine.
I stare up at the awards and accolades
that line my walls.
But I feel detached, untethered.
I am a stranger
in the home, in the country
where I once thought I belonged.

Máire fusses over me.
*Oh God Don,*
*I can't bear to see you like this.*
*Will we go out for a walk?*
*A bit of fresh air*
*will blow away the cobwebs.*

*Well Máire,* I say,
*perhaps you could take me*
*to the sand dune of my birth.*

*Show me the scene*
*of the shell squashing crime?*

*Oh for God's sake Don!* says Máire.
*The past is the past.*
*It'll do you no good*
*getting all nostalgic like that.*
It is then that I realise
even my own mother
is sick of my melancholy chicken shit.

We're shooting McDonagh's *Chicken Run*
in an actual chicken farm.
They're planning to use the farm birds
as extras – it's cheaper that way.
*Happy Egg Hill* is the name of the place.
It's only ten minutes down the road
from Máire and Declan
which is handy when they want you
in the makeup chair at four a.m.
I invite Máire to come on set with me
to see where the magic happens.
But she refuses
*Oh no no no,*
*no thanks Don,*
*I couldn't possibly.*

I'm not quite sure
what I was expecting
that first morning
at *Happy Egg Hill.*
Perhaps a jolly farmer
in some yellow wellies
or a grassy green glade
full of contented hens grazing.
Instead, a huge concrete monolith
reminiscent of an Amazon dispatch centre,
towers above me.

Martin McDonagh greets me.
Shakes my wing
just a little too hard.
*Alright Don,*
*are you ready for the shoot?*
*It's gonna be tough.*
*I hope you can stomach it.*

I am escorted to my trailer
where we are encouraged to remain
between scenes.
There is to be strictly no wandering
of *Happy Egg Hill* unaccompanied.
There was an incident yesterday,

Brendan Gleeson

walked into the wrong barn

and fainted.

There are rumbles of

animal rights activists

disrupting the shoot.

*The last thing that we need now*

*is PETA in here,*

*down on top of Martin*

*like a ton of bricks*

*impeding his art!* says the first AD,

as she locks my trailer

with me inside.

The manic cries of feral hens

bleed through my trailer walls.

Not even my noise-cancelling headphones

can drown them out.

I have never been so desperate

for a line of ket

and its annihilating bliss.

I text Colin,

*Hey man, any bag?*

But he doesn't reply.

Rude.

So I decide to track him down

in person.

I use my trusty ket key

to break out of my trailer.

*Happy Egg Hill* is a sea

of concrete barns and dimly lit corridors.

But it is strangely familiar

to me, somehow,

and on autopilot

I veer towards a set of double doors

labelled *Sexing Room.*

I push them open.

Inside zombie workers

stand like pillars

between trays and trays

of newborn chicks.

Their tiny baby eyes are blinking

under blinding lights.

I stare transfixed

as the workers fish out the male chicks

and fling them onto a conveyor belt

leading towards a boxy metallic machine

reminiscent of...

a sausage meat grinder.

My vision blurs.

The déjà vu of it

punches me in the chicken gut.

Suddenly I am tumbling back in time,

I am a seconds-old chick again.

My tiny baby body

being probed by gloved hands.

Ahead of me, my newborn brothers

are tossed to the conveyor belt

and I am next!

I am trundling to my demise

like Sadie's sacrificial egg.

Seconds from death

I am swooped to safety.

I look up to see

two big brown human eyes

and a terrible 90s perm,

under a factory hairnet.

It's none other

than my future surrogate mother

Máire Murphy.

*Don't worry chick,* she says

*I'm going to get you out of here.*

She pockets me

and it all goes black.

I come to,

dizzy,

dazed,

gasping for air.

I stagger backwards

in search of the exit

but in my frenzy

I fall through another set of double doors.

My feathered friends,

the sight that meets my eyes

can only be described as akin

to the Versace summer sample sale

in hell.

Thousands of hens cover

every square inch of barn floor.

They're henpecked, panicked.

They rush around

like headless chickens,

bearing bloody bald patches.

Their manic stares

bore holes in my flesh.

But for the first time in my life

I am alive to their plight.

Their pain is my pain.

My consciousness cracks open like an egg

and it dawns on me...

it is my destiny

to set these chickens free.

Liberty!

Ecstasy!

Pure unadulterated feathered chaos!

An alarm sounds.

Workers appear

bearing brooms and batons.

But I am unafraid.

Feather to feather

with my winged family,

we stand them down.

Sadie's words echo in my ears,

*We gotta put our bodies on the line baby.*

*This is how we win!*

*COME AT ME YOU MURDERING BASTARDS!*

> *Triumphant classical music plays.* **DON** *leaps around in cockfight mode. He yanks out his feathers in exhilaration. He kicks, kaws, screeches, pulls down his chicken pants and peels off his jacket, revealing his pimply chicken skin underneath.*

Martin McDonagh appears,

his director chair

is folded over his shoulder

like a gun

but I am unafraid.

*Are you ready for your close-up Martin?*

> **DON** *lunges toward Martin ready to attack,*
> *but gets smacked in the head and crumples*
> *to the floor.*

> *A beat as* **DON** *comes to. Smoke begins to fill*
> *the room.*

Well my feathered friends

here we find ourselves.

Cosy,

claustrophobic,

almost like...

chickens in a coop.

Like many risings before

ours was doomed to fail

and now we must face

the firing squad together.

The air is thin,

hard to breathe

if you think about it for too long.

Sometimes I feel as though

I am losing my grip on reality.

But one thing is certain,

death is just around the corner.

But there is such strength in solidarity

my feathered friends.

I have never been so proud to perch

wing to wing with you.

Although our deaths

will go undocumented,

we know in the final hour

we rose up and fought

for the rights of all birds

to fly free.

I think now of my great namesake,

Daniel O'Connell.

I have failed to be a liberator,

I am no hero.

But I am a proud Irish man,

I am Declan's son.

And most of all

just like you...

I am a chicken!

**End**

9 780573 000539